Ripley's MIGHTY MACHINES

Believe It or Not!®

RIPLEY PUBLISHING

a Jim Pattison Company

TWISTS

Written by Ian Graham
Consultant Chris Oxlade

RIPLEY
PUBLISHING

Publisher Anne Marshall

Managing Editor Rebecca Miles
Picture Researcher James Proud
Editors Lisa Regan, Rosie Alexander, Charlotte Howell
Proofreader Judy Barratt
Indexer Hilary Bird

Art Director Sam South
Design Rocket Design (East Anglia) Ltd
Reprographics Juice Creative Ltd

www.ripleybooks.com

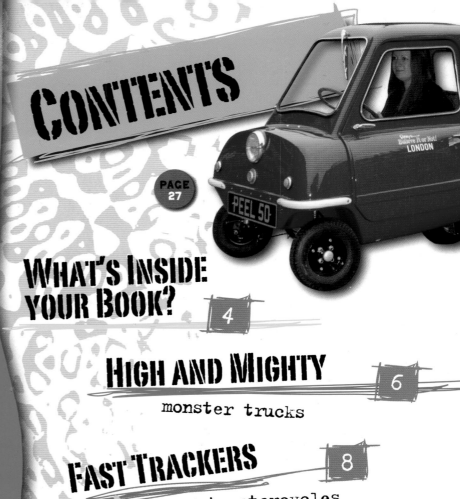

CONTENTS

PAGE 27

TWISTS

PAGE 25

MEAN MACHINES on the move

Feeling the need for speed? Wish your dad's car was bigger than anyone else's? Or perhaps robots are more your thing? Humans have invented some mighty machines that let us go faster than ever before, reach other planets, soar through the skies, or simply attract attention from unsuspecting passers-by.

Take a trip around your favourite mechanical and moving things with this fun but factual book. Learn about the science of flight, put some wind in your sails, and boost your va-va-voom with special Ripley's fascinating facts and amazing 'Believe It or Not!' stories from around the world. What are you waiting for? Off you go!

WHAT'S INSIDE YOUR BOOK?

Monster Trucks first became popular in the 1970s. The Monster Truck Racing Association, formed in 1988, set down standard rules about safety and construction. These days, Monster Truck shows make millions of dollars.

Learn fab fast facts to go with the cool pictures.

In 1974 a Monster Truck called Bigfoot (see page 6) was the first Monster Truck to drive over cars and crush them.

Big as they are, Monster Trucks can perform cool stunts such as wheelstands, jumps and doughnuts.

TWISTS

Don't forget to look out for the 'twist it!' column on some pages. Twist the book to find out more fast facts about mighty machines.

A small boat is fun to sail, but a big racing yacht is one of the most exciting ways to travel. Racing yachts can slice through the waves at 55 km/h. Super yachts more than 30 m long can go even faster. A few of the 50,000 ships that carry goods and materials around the world have been built with sails too. Using wind power instead of engines saves fuel.

ur boat doesn't have engine, you could roll your sleeves and row or you could hoist a ail and let the wind do the work.

nd power

Each mast is 50 m tall.

The sails are made from a strong synthetic fabric and cover an area of 2,500 sq m.

The ship is 187 m long, 20 m wide and weighs nearly 15,000 tonnes.

carry 308 passengers and has seven decks.

>> PLAIN SAILING >>

French vet Raphaela Le Gouvello crossed the Indian Ocean on a sailboard just 8 m long and 1.2 m wide. The 6,300-km journey took 60 days. Raphaela spent eight hours a day at the sail. She has also crossed the Atlantic and Pacific Oceans and the Mediterranean Sea by sailboard.

WATER WAYS

Japanese sailor Kenichi Horie spent three months sailing alone across the Pacific Ocean on a yacht made from beer barrels.

British woman Hilary Lister sailed across the English Channel between England and France in August 2005, even though she could not move her arms or legs. She steered her yacht by sucking and blowing through tubes that operated the rudder and sails.

During a round-the-world voyage in 1997, British yachtsman Tony Bullimore survived for five days underneath his capsized yacht in the icy Southern Ocean until help arrived.

When a Russian yacht lost its rudder in the Southern Ocean in 2005, the crew replaced it with a cabin door.

twist it!

BIG WORD ALERT!

CAPSIZED

Upturned. A capsized boat is one that has rolled upside-down.

Ripley explains...

A yacht sail works like an aircraft wing. When a sail fills with air, it forms the same curved shape as a wing. This changes the flow of air to create low pressure. The low pressure pulls the boat along. It can move a yacht in a different direction from the wind by setting the sails at the correct angle.

Even enormous cargo ships can be wind powered. SkySails are huge computer-controlled kites that give extra power and help save fuel.

CLOSE TO THE WIND

The Wind Surf is a cruise liner that can be powered by either computer-controlled sails or engines. Its sails unfurl automatically from the 50-m-tall masts within two minutes of pushing a button on the ship's bridge. Using only sails, its top speed is about 24 km/h, about the same as its maximum speed on engine power.

Ripley's Believe It or Not!

BRICK BOAT

It took Peter Lange from New Zealand three months to build his 6-m-long brick boat using 676 bricks. Amazingly, it didn't sink!

Do the twist

This book is packed with amazing mechanical devices. It will teach you cool things about all kinds of machines, but like all Twists books, it shines a spotlight on things that are unbelievable but true. Turn the pages and find out more...

FASCINATING FACT! FASCINATING FACT! FASCINATING FACT!

Look for the Ripley R to find out even more than you knew before!

Twists are all about Believe It or Not: amazing facts, feats and things that will make you go 'Wow!'.

Found a new word? Big word alerts will explain it for you.

HIGH AND MIGHTY

monster trucks

Bigfoot 5 stands nearly 5 m high.

They're massive and mean. They leap in the air and flatten cars. No, they're not flying elephants, they're Monster Trucks. These mechanical giants are the stars of stunt-driving shows that never fail to wow the crowds. A roaring 2,000-horsepower engine gives them a top speed of 160 km/h.

In the hands of an expert driver, they can spin on the spot, rear up on their back wheels and jump nearly 8 m off the ground. But don't get in their way. They weigh more than 4 tonnes and they can crush a car so that it's as flat as a pancake.

MEET BIGFOOT 5

Bigfoot 5's giant tyres were originally made for the US Army for use on an Arctic snow train. The tyres ended up in a junkyard where builder Bob Chandler found them and transformed them into Bigfoot 5's weapons of destruction. At 3 m high, the tyres are the largest on any truck. Monster Trucks get to crush about 3,000 junkyard cars in shows every year.

it's home!

Sheikh Hamad Bin Hamdan Al Nahyan, from the United Arab Emirates, is a collector of awesome automobiles, including this towering power wagon, the biggest in the world, complete with air-conditioned bedrooms, lounge, bathroom, kitchen, and patio area in the back.

A harness holds the driver safely in the driving seat.

The body is from a 1996 pick-up truck.

It is powered by a monster 7.5-litre engine.

Each of the wheels weighs more than a tonne.

CRAZY

Monster Trucks can jump nearly 8 m high and a distance of 40 m – about the same as 14 cars parked side by side.

If you want to buy your own Monster Truck, it will cost you about £100,000.

It costs about £165,000 a year to run a Monster Truck team.

Don't get a puncture – a new tyre will cost you £1,700.

Monster Trucks are thirsty. They burn 9.5 litres of fuel in each run of about 76 m – that's 1,000 times faster than a car would burn the same amount of fuel.

THAT'S IT!

magnificent motorcycles

Millions of bikers can't be wrong. Two wheels and an engine mean lots of fun. Motorbikes have been around for more than 120 years and they're still as popular as ever. There are motorbikes for riding to work, motorbikes for dirt tracks, motorbikes for looking cool and motorbikes for racing. They're all different.

The strangest are the motorbikes that are specially made for setting speed records. They look like two-wheeled rockets. On 26 September 2008, Rocky Robinson rode one of these crazy machines, called Ack Attack, at a speed of 580.833 km/h. That's nearly twice as fast as a Formula 1 racing car.

power machine!

The Dodge Tomahawk has a huge 8.3-litre engine from a Dodge Viper supercar – that's four or five times bigger than most car engines. The designers think it has a top speed of about 480 km/h, but no one has ever been brave enough to try riding it that fast. Only ten Tomahawks have been built and, if you want one, it will cost about £375,000. Even then you won't be able to ride it on public roads.

A BARGAIN, ONLY £375,000!

8.3 litre engine is also used in supercars.

CUTTING EDGE

Why stop at one engine? This motorbike is powered by no less than 24 chainsaw engines. It's nearly 4 m long and can reach a top speed of 255 km/h.

Dead cool

Gordon Fitch has created a fitting last ride for keen bikers in Britain. They can have their coffins drawn by a Harley Davidson motorbike.

BIKER BEDLAM

In 2004, Indian magician O.P. Sharma rode a motorcycle down a busy street in the city of Patna with a black bag over his head. Don't try this at home!

German tightrope artist Johann Traber rode a motorcycle on a high-wire 160 m above the Rhine River in 2003. His father, also called Johann, sat on a trapeze hanging below the bike during the 579-m crossing.

Gregory Frazier of Fort Smith, Montana, has ridden around the world on a motorcycle five times. He's covered over 1.6 million km.

In 2004, U.S. motorcycle stuntman Robbie Knievel (son of the famous daredevil Evel Knievel) made a spectacular 55-m jump over two helicopters and five aeroplanes parked on the deck of the Intrepid Museum, an aircraft-carrier-turned-museum in Manhattan, New York.

twist it!

Engine air intake.

Double wheels front and back spread the massive weight.

Special rim brakes.

SOMETHING'S MISSING

Ben Gulak in Toronto, Canada, sits atop his fast-track invention – Uno, the world's first one-wheeled motorbike. To give the ride more stability, Ben put the wheels side-by-side just 2 cm apart and directly under the rider, who accelerates by leaning forward. When the rider leans into a turn, the inside wheel lifts and the outside wheel lowers, so both stay firmly on the ground. What's even more unusual about the bike is that it's all-electric, emitting no fumes.

PEDAL POWER
on your bike!

Bicycles aren't very big or fast, but they are mighty machines. A bike's diamond-shaped frame is so strong that it can carry more than ten times its own weight. It has no engine, but can keep going for thousands of kilometres – as long as you keep pushing the pedals.

It's sometimes hard enough to ride a bike with two wheels without falling over, but could you balance on just one wheel? Some people actually enjoy riding a one-wheeled machine called a unicycle. You need a really good sense of balance.

FASCINATING FACT!

Chris Hoy from Scotland is surely the most successful sprint cyclist of all time. By the age of 32, he had accumulated the following titles (among others): 🏅 Four times Olympic Champion 🏅 Olympic Silver 🏅 Olympic Team Sprint Record 🏅 World Record 500 m 🏅 European Champion 🏅 Nine times World Champion 🏅 27 times World Cup Gold

Built for speed

The best track bikes are built for speed. Their weight is cut down as much as possible, because heavier bikes are harder to get moving. Anything that might stick out, catch the air and slow the bike down is smoothed out. The bike's body is made in one piece.

The bars are low to make the rider bend forwards into the right position for good aerodynamics.

The seat is set high to get maximum power from the legs.

Four or five broad spokes stir up less air than thin wire spokes.

Skinny, low-drag tyres.

There are no brakes – they are not needed!

The back wheel is solid, because it slips through the air easily.

PEDAL MEDALS

In 2005, Sam Wakeling rode his unicycle the length of Britain, a distance of 1,406 km.

In May 2007, Quinn Baumberger set out on a nine-month bike journey the length of the Americas, from Alaska to Argentina. He covered 30,600 km and had 50 flat tyres on the way.

The first two-wheeler was built by Baron Karl von Drais in Germany in 1817. It was called a 'draisine' after the Baron. There were no pedals. The rider sat astride it and pushed it along with his feet.

In the 1860s, bikes were called boneshakers because their wooden or metal wheels rattled and bumped over rough cobbled streets.

Twelve cyclists rode 900 km across New Zealand's South Island in 15 days on unicycles.

Frenchman Hughes Richard climbed the 747 steps of the Eiffel Tower on a bicycle in just 19 minutes in April 2002.

Christian Adam of Germany can ride a bicycle backwards while playing a violin.

twist it!

It's hard enough to ride a bike in the usual way, but Dutchman Pieter de Hart can ride a bike while sitting on the handlebars and also facing backwards! In 2002, he cycled 27 km like this.

THINK SMALL!

Bobby Hunt rides this tiny bike in his stage act. It measures only 7.6 cm from the middle of the front wheel to the middle of the back wheel, and it's only 20 cm tall.

Wheely fast!

In 2008, Mark Beaumont became the fastest man to ride around the world, taking just 195 days to pedal 29,446 km and smashing the previous attempt by 81 days.

MAGNIFICENT MOTORS

cool cars

It's hard to imagine our world without cars. There are about 700 million of them worldwide – so it's no wonder the roads get jammed sometimes. A few of these millions of cars are special. They are designed to be very fast, or very small, or just very silly.

Cars have been made in all sorts of surprising shapes and sizes. If you fancy driving a car in the shape of an armchair or a hamburger, the chances are that someone, somewhere, has made a car to make your wish come true.

Awesome

The **Bugatti Veyron** is one of the fastest cars in the world. It has a top speed of more than 400 km/h. That's faster than a racing car or an express train.

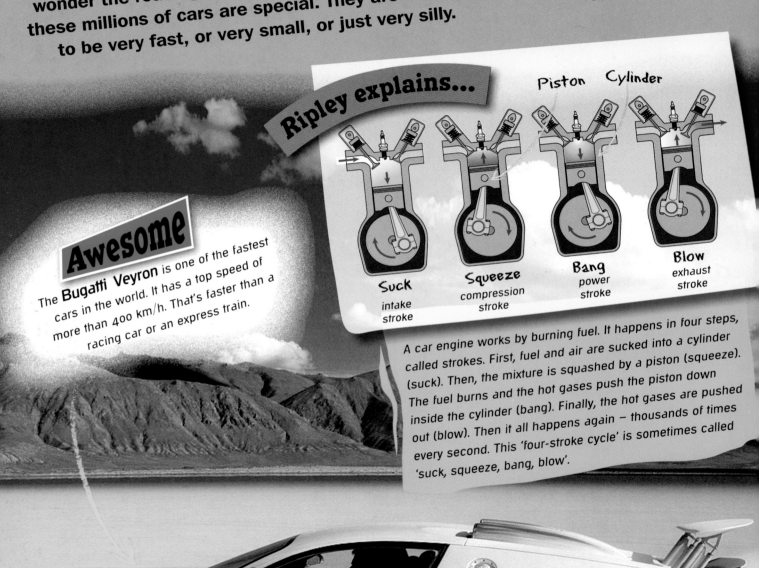

Ripley explains...

Piston   Cylinder

Suck
intake
stroke

Squeeze
compression
stroke

Bang
power
stroke

Blow
exhaust
stroke

A car engine works by burning fuel. It happens in four steps, called strokes. First, fuel and air are sucked into a cylinder (suck). Then, the mixture is squashed by a piston (squeeze). The fuel burns and the hot gases push the piston down inside the cylinder (bang). Finally, the hot gases are pushed out (blow). Then it all happens again – thousands of times every second. This 'four-stroke cycle' is sometimes called 'suck, squeeze, bang, blow'.

twist it!

This couch is no slouch! It can reach a speed of 140 km/h, being powered by a 1.3-litre engine. It is steered with a pizza pan!

A single day's consumption of electricity in the USA is enough to power a car more than 36,000 times around the world.

Kenneth L. Moorhouse designed and built a working car only 1.3 m long and 86 cm wide, with a top speed of more than 200 km/h.

Edd China invented the 'office car', an office desk and chair that can be driven like a car. In 2003, it set out from London, England, on a 1,500-km charity road-trip to the south of France.

The first motor race, from Paris to Rouen in 1894, was won by Count de Dion with an average speed of about 19 km/h. An athlete can run faster than this!

DIVER DRIVER

Frank Rinderknecht loves to go for a drive... in the sea! His submersible car, called 'sQuba', can drive on land or underwater. The car flies through the water at a depth of 10 m, whilst the driver and passenger breathe compressed air. Instead of a four-stroke combustion engine, the car is powered by electric motors.

transformers!

Brazilian Olisio da Silva and his two sons, Marco and Marcus, have created a real-life transformer. Their Kia Besta van takes just six minutes to morph into a 3.65-m-high robot, accompanied by thumping music, smoke and flashing lights. It took them nine months and £84,000 to create the 'SuperRoboCar'.

THE CAR'S THE STAR

The Bugatti Veyron is one of the world's most expensive cars. Each one costs about a million pounds.

The Veyron's engine is in the middle of the car, behind the driver.

The amazing engine is over six times more powerful than a family car engine.

Two pipes on the roof, called snorkels, lead air down into the engine.

When the car reaches a speed of 220 km/h, a wing-like spoiler unfolds from the back.

WACKY RACERS

out of the ordinary

Motor racing is amazingly popular. In the USA, seven million fans watch each NASCAR race. Every Formula 1 race has 55 million people glued to their television screens all over the world.

But 'ordinary' motor racing just isn't enough for some people. They can't look at a lawnmower or a snowmobile without wondering how fast it can go. It isn't long before they're racing each other. You name it, and someone has raced it. Almost anything can have an engine and wheels bolted on for a race. Beds, barrels and even toilets have been turned into wacky racing machines.

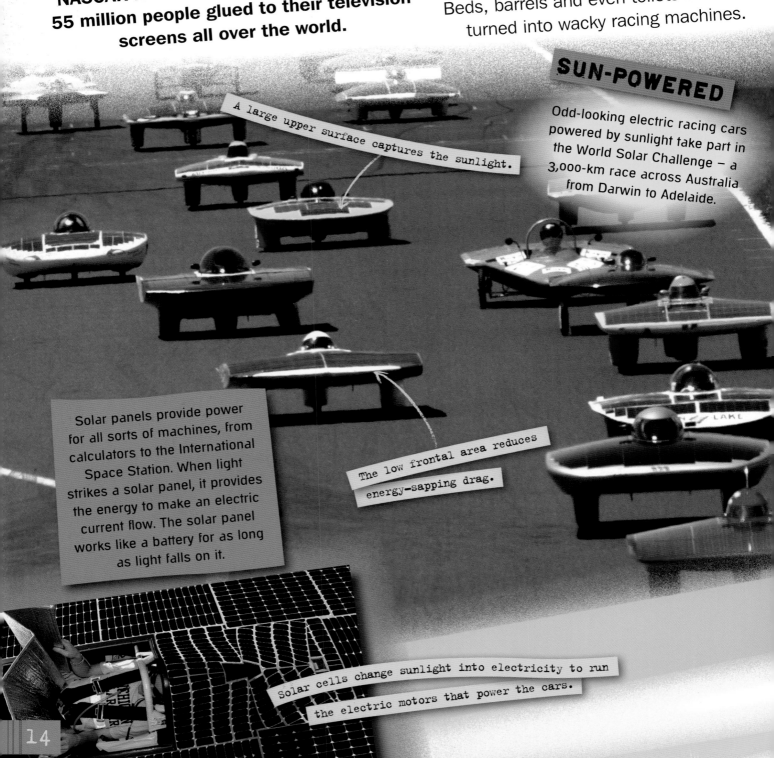

SUN-POWERED

Odd-looking electric racing cars powered by sunlight take part in the World Solar Challenge – a 3,000-km race across Australia from Darwin to Adelaide.

A large upper surface captures the sunlight.

Solar panels provide power for all sorts of machines, from calculators to the International Space Station. When light strikes a solar panel, it provides the energy to make an electric current flow. The solar panel works like a battery for as long as light falls on it.

The low frontal area reduces energy-sapping drag.

Solar cells change sunlight into electricity to run the electric motors that power the cars.

RACING AROUND

The National Lawnmower Racing Championships in Mendota, Illinois, started as an April Fool's joke in 1992, but proved so popular that it became an annual event.

The annual Furniture Race in Whitefish, Montana, involves competitors attaching skis to various items of furniture and racing them down the nearby Big Mountain.

Every year, bed-racing enthusiasts flock to Arizona for the annual Oatman Bed Race. The teams push their beds down the main street, make the beds and then race back to the finish line to the sound of the Chamber Pot Band.

Here's a tale. Emma Crawford was buried on top of Red Mountain, Colorado, in 1891, but her coffin slid down the Canyon in 1929 after heavy rains. Now, as a bizarre form of action replay, every year in nearby Manitou Springs, teams build and race coffins with a living female occupant.

twist it!

These daredevil racers reach 20 km/h on their motorised beer barrels in Windsor, England.

>> chair-raising! >>

Sixty-four participants took part in the Office Chair World Championships, which took place in Olten, Switzerland. Racers sped downhill over 200 m, hurtling over ramps and jumps.

BIG WORD ALERT!

NASCAR
A type of motor racing in the USA.

FORMULA I
A motor-racing championship in single-seat racing cars. Races take place all over the world.

Joel King's jet-powered street luge board can reach 180 km/h. The board has no brakes – he stops by putting his feet down. Ouch!

PRIVATE TRANSPORTERS

just for one

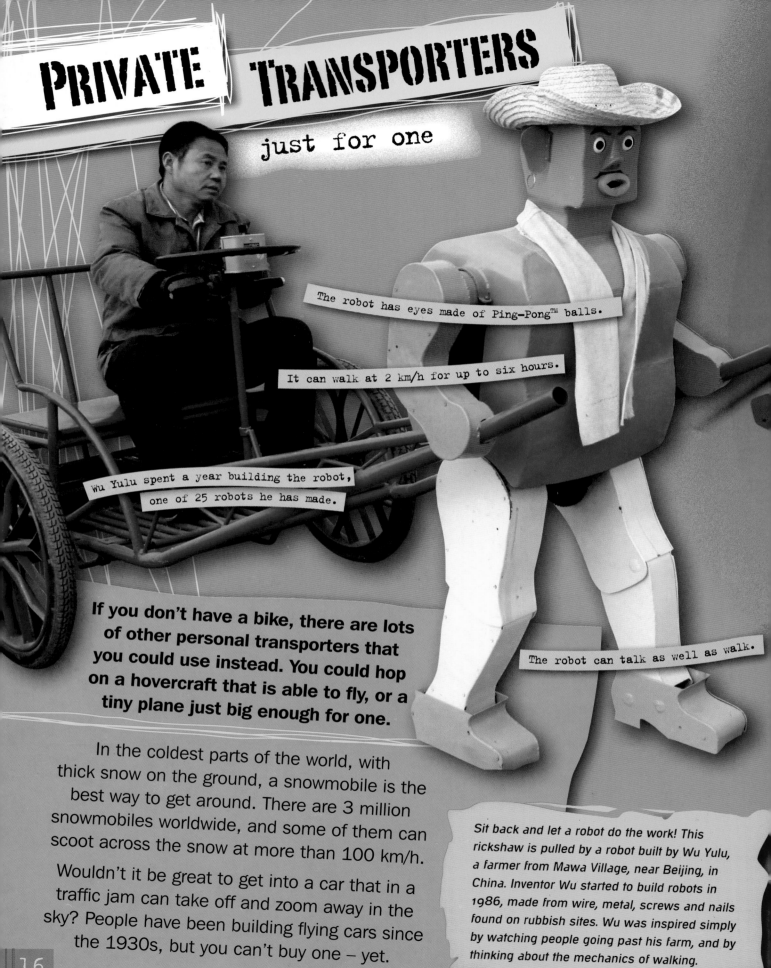

The robot has eyes made of Ping-Pong™ balls.

It can walk at 2 km/h for up to six hours.

Wu Yulu spent a year building the robot, one of 25 robots he has made.

The robot can talk as well as walk.

If you don't have a bike, there are lots of other personal transporters that you could use instead. You could hop on a hovercraft that is able to fly, or a tiny plane just big enough for one.

In the coldest parts of the world, with thick snow on the ground, a snowmobile is the best way to get around. There are 3 million snowmobiles worldwide, and some of them can scoot across the snow at more than 100 km/h.

Wouldn't it be great to get into a car that in a traffic jam can take off and zoom away in the sky? People have been building flying cars since the 1930s, but you can't buy one – yet.

Sit back and let a robot do the work! This rickshaw is pulled by a robot built by Wu Yulu, a farmer from Mawa Village, near Beijing, in China. Inventor Wu started to build robots in 1986, made from wire, metal, screws and nails found on rubbish sites. Wu was inspired simply by watching people going past his farm, and by thinking about the mechanics of walking.

Greg Kolodziejzyk has pure pedal power. In 2006, on a racetrack in California, he cycled a mammoth 1,041 km in 24 hours and clocked up the fastest time ever for pedalling 1,000 km – he took just 23 hours 2 minutes. His Critical Power bike is no ordinary two-wheeler. He rides it lying down. It can reach speeds of 100 km/h and has a cruising speed of 50 km/h on a flat road.

Gamini Wasnatha Kumara pulled a 40-tonne railway carriage 25 m in Colombo, Sri Lanka, in 2001, by means of a rope gripped between his teeth.

PHEW!

Eleven-year-old Bruce Khlebnikov towed a plane with a rope attached to his hair on 24 May 2001, in Moscow, Russia.

In 1909, Walter Flexenberger invented the Sea Cycle, a catamaran powered by a paddlewheel turned by pedalling a bicycle.

In 2000, 20 men pulled a dump truck around a car park in Kenosha, Wisconsin, for an hour non-stop, covering a distance of 5 km.

In 2005, Zhang Xingquan from China not only pulled a family car using his ear, he did it while walking on raw eggs – without breaking them.

In 2006, 72-year-old Chinese grandmother Wang Xiaobei pulled a truck loaded with people for 10 m – with her teeth!

FAST IT!

In Beijing a group of people demonstrate how pedal power can generate electricity that can be stored in portable rechargeable batteries. The batteries are then able to power electrical appliances, such as washing machines.

PUSH HEEL IN

DID YOU KNOW?

The first submarines were human-powered. In 1620, a Dutchman, Cornelis Drebbel, designed a wooden vehicle encased in leather. It was able to carry 12 rowers and a total of 20 men. Amazingly, the vessel could dive to a depth of 5 m and travel 10 km. The crew turned the propeller by hand.

CRAZY TRANSPORT

far out!

If you're bored with travelling in the usual ways, there are some more exciting ways to get around.

Those of you who are really brave could try being fired out of a circus cannon. You could fly 45 m through the air at up to 80 km/h. Or take a leaf out of Felix Baumgartner's book. In 2003, he strapped a 1.8-m wing to his back and jumped out of a plane. He glided 35 km from England to France across the English Channel. You could try fitting rockets to a car, or a jet engine to a boat. Jet-powered racing boats, called hydroplanes, can reach speeds of more than 350 km/h.

LED

In-suit drink bag.

Oxygen and temperature controls.

The SAFER pack attaches to the bottom of a normal space backpack.

>>UP, UP AND AWAY>>

NASA insists that astronauts from the space shuttle or International Space Station wear a SAFER jet pack for spacewalks. If they drift away from the spacecraft, they can use it to fly back to safety. Crazily they fly through space, miles from Earth.

FASCINATING FACT! FASCINATING FACT!

SAFER JET-PACK

SAFER stands for Simplified Aid For EVA Rescue. It works by sending out jets of nitrogen gas. There are 24 jets pointing in three different directions (up and down, backwards and forwards, and side to side). By choosing which jets to use, the astronaut can vary his or her direction.

BIG WORD ALERT!

NASA

The National Aeronautics and Space Administration – the organisation that carries out space exploration for the USA.

On 5 March 2005, 47 people went surfing on Australia's Gold Coast on a single massive surfboard measuring 12 m long and 3 m wide.

Tim Arfons gets around on a jet-powered bar stool. The stool reached speeds of 64 km/h at a raceway in Norwalk, Ohio.

In 2006, two British women, Antonia Bolingbroke-Kent and Jo Huxster, drove a three-wheel taxi, called a tuk-tuk, 19,000 km from Thailand to England through 12 countries.

twist it!

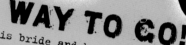

WAY TO GO!

This bride and her bridesmaids rode to her wedding in a tractor bucket in China in 2008. The groom arrived in his own tractor bucket, also decorated with balloons.

David Smith, from Missouri, USA, used a cannon to fire himself across the US/Mexican border. He waved his passport as he flew past customs control.

Paul Stender's Port-O-Jet consists of a wooden washroom hut powered by a 50-year-old, 340-kg Boeing jet engine. It travels at 74 km/h and throws 10-m fireballs from the burner at the back. He drives it while seated on the original toilet inside.

LITTLE AND LARGE

extreme vehicles

Did you know that you can stretch a car and make it longer? Not like a rubber band – a stretch limo is a luxury car made longer by cutting it in two and putting an extra section in the middle. Whereas an ordinary car is 4 or 5 m long, stretch limos are usually about 8.5 m, but the world's longest is 30.5 m long. However, some people think that small is beautiful. The tiniest cars are less than 1 m high, and the most minuscule planes are just 4 m long. That's about the same length as a car.

Driven mad

Gregory Denham from California, USA, poses at the wheel of his Dream Big motorbike. Rumoured to be the biggest motorbike in the world, it stands a whopping 3.35 m high and 6.2 m long. Denham wanted a bike that could perform like a Monster Truck, so he went ahead and built one!

ROOM FOR EVERYONE

Meet one long, long limo, made by Jay Ohrberg – known as 'The King of Show Cars'. This lengthy motor is 30 m long and has a helicopter landing site at the back. Add some friends... and drive!

Room for one

The Bede BD-5J is a 4-m-long plane, powered by a tiny jet engine with a top speed of 483 km/h. With room enough for just one, it was piloted by 007 in the James Bond film *Octopussy*.

Let's compare...

The titchy Bede BD-5J with the world's biggest airliner, the Airbus A380

AIRBUS A380 | A380

	Height	Length	Max weight	Wingspan	Max speed
Bede BD-5J	1.7 m	3.7 m	385 kg	5.2 m	483 km/h
Airbus A380	24.1 m	73 m	560,000 kg	79.8 m	945 km/h

Check out the bags of lead shot, designed to keep the nose down.

For more on the Airbus A380, turn to page 40.

twist it!

Benji Ming, at the Edinburgh Festival, Scotland, was so enraged at the small audiences he was attracting for his shows that he transferred his performances from the theatre to the confines of a Smart car. He delivered a comic monologue to a packed house – an audience of one in the passenger seat.

Twenty-one Malaysian students crammed themselves into a Mini Cooper in June 2006.

Jasper, a black Doberman–Labrador owned by Sir Benjamin Slade in England, travels everywhere by stretch limo.

EXTREME!

Streeeetch!

There's room to be creative with the interiors in this 12-m-long Hummer, owned by Scott Demaret from Bristol, England.

SMALL IS BEAUTIFUL

Designed to seat one person and a shopping bag, the Peel P50 was a three-wheeled micro-car, first produced in 1963. It had one door, a single windscreen wiper and only one headlight. With vital statistics of just 134 cm by 99 cm, its minuscule frame weighed in at only 59 kg, but could manage a speed of 61 km/h. Handy for slipping into that confined parking space, the Peel had just one drawback – no reverse gear!

PEEL 50

Ripley's Believe It or Not! LONDON

ROBOTS ARE REAL!

The robots are coming! Robots in films are often walking, talking machines that look like metal people. Real robots are often not quite so lifelike, but there are more than six million robots in the world today.

man machines

A million of them are industrial robots. These are computer-controlled arms that help to make things in factories. The other five million or so are service robots. These include robot toys, vacuum cleaners and lawnmowers. Honda's ASIMO robot (see far right) is a real walking, talking humanlike robot. ASIMO is 1.3 m tall and weighs 54 kg. It can walk at 2.5 km/h and even run a little faster.

The word robot was used for the first time in a theatre play called Rossum's Universal Robots by the Czech writer Karel Capek in 1921.

6-m-long flames shoot from its nostrils.

Mighty muncher

Its jaws crush with a force of 9,000 kg — powerful enough to bite a car in two.

Robosaurus is a 12-m-tall robot that can lift, crush, burn and bite. Created by American inventor Doug Malewicki, it's as high as a five-storey building and is controlled by a human pilot strapped inside the monster's head. As flames jet out of its nostrils, its jaws can tear into a car, ripping it in two.

A large truck engine in the tail powers the beast.

Robosaurus weighs 26 tonnes.

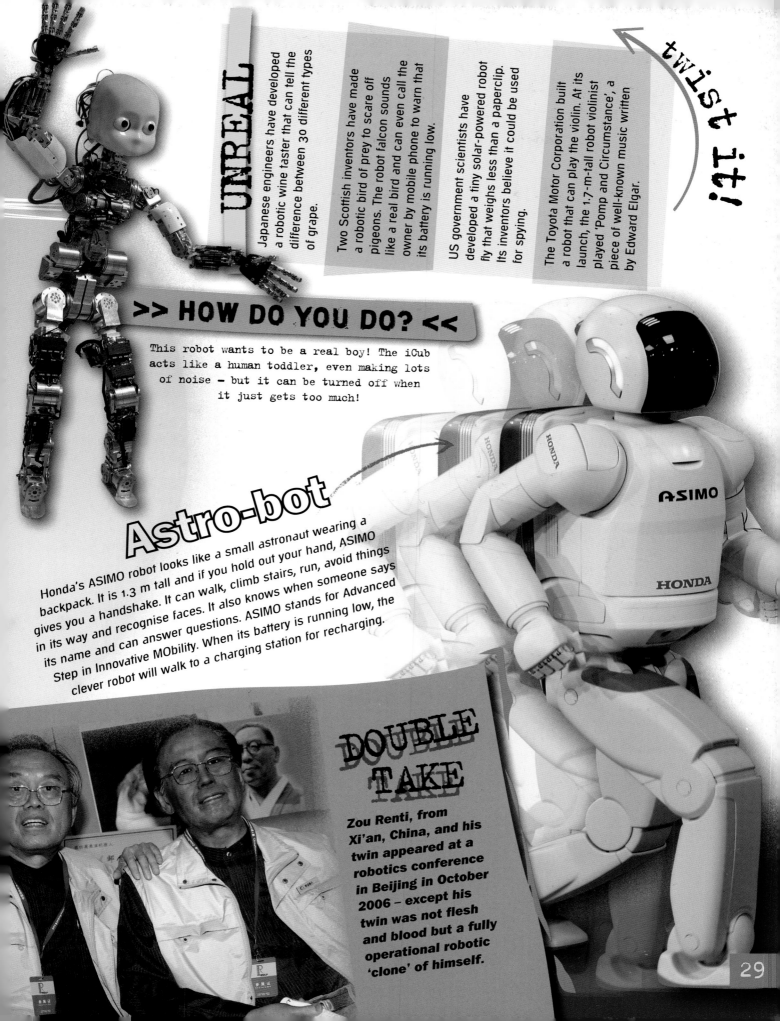

UNREAL

Japanese engineers have developed a robotic wine taster that can tell the difference between 30 different types of grape.

Two Scottish inventors have made a robotic bird of prey to scare off pigeons. The robot falcon sounds like a real bird and can even call the owner by mobile phone to warn that its battery is running low.

US government scientists have developed a tiny solar-powered robot fly that weighs less than a paperclip. Its inventors believe it could be used for spying.

The Toyota Motor Corporation built a robot that can play the violin. At its launch, the 1.7-m-tall robot violinist played 'Pomp and Circumstance', a piece of well-known music written by Edward Elgar.

>> HOW DO YOU DO? <<

This robot wants to be a real boy! The iCub acts like a human toddler, even making lots of noise — but it can be turned off when it just gets too much!

Astro-bot

Honda's ASIMO robot looks like a small astronaut wearing a backpack. It is 1.3 m tall and if you hold out your hand, ASIMO gives you a handshake. It can walk, climb stairs, run, avoid things in its way and recognise faces. It also knows when someone says its name and can answer questions. ASIMO stands for Advanced Step in Innovative MObility. When its battery is running low, the clever robot will walk to a charging station for recharging.

DOUBLE TAKE

Zou Renti, from Xi'an, China, and his twin appeared at a robotics conference in Beijing in October 2006 – except his twin was not flesh and blood but a fully operational robotic 'clone' of himself.

FOR SAIL

If your boat doesn't have an engine, you could roll up your sleeves and row it, or you could hoist a sail and let the wind do the work.

wind power

A small boat is fun to sail, but a big racing yacht is one of the most exciting ways to travel. Racing yachts can slice through the waves at 55 km/h. Super yachts more than 30 m long can go even faster. A few of the 50,000 ships that carry goods and materials around the world have been built with sails too. Using wind power instead of engines saves fuel.

Each mast is 50 m tall.

The sails are made from a strong synthetic fabric and cover an area of 2,500 sq m.

The ship can carry 308 passengers and has seven decks.

BELUGA PROJECTS

powered by SkySails

Even enormous cargo ships can be wind powered. SkySails are huge computer-controlled kites that give extra power and help save fuel.

CLOSE TO THE WIND

The Wind Surf is a cruise liner that can be powered by either computer-controlled sails or engines. Its sails unfurl automatically from the 50-m-tall masts within two minutes of pushing a button on the ship's bridge. Using only sails, its top speed is about 24 km/h, about the same as its maximum speed on engine power.

French vet Raphaela Le Gouvello crossed the Indian Ocean on a sailboard just 8 m long and 1.2 m wide. The 6,300-km journey took 60 days. Raphaela spent eight hours a day at the sail. She has also crossed the Atlantic and Pacific Oceans and the Mediterranean Sea by sailboard.

The ship is 187 m long, 20 m wide and weighs nearly 15,000 tonnes.

WATER WAYS

Japanese sailor Kenichi Horie spent three months sailing alone across the Pacific Ocean on a yacht made from beer barrels.

British woman Hilary Lister sailed across the English Channel between England and France in August 2005, even though she could not move her arms or legs. She steered her yacht by sucking and blowing through tubes that operated the rudder and sails.

During a round-the-world voyage in 1997, British yachtsman Tony Bullimore survived for five days underneath his capsized yacht in the icy Southern Ocean until help arrived.

When a Russian yacht lost its rudder in the Southern Ocean in 2005, the crew replaced it with a cabin door.

twist it!

BIG WORD ALERT!

CAPSIZED

Upturned. A capsized boat is one that has rolled upside-down.

Ripley's Believe It or Not!®

BRICK BOAT

It took Peter Lange from New Zealand three months to build his 6-m-long brick boat using 676 bricks. Amazingly, it didn't sink!

Ripley explains...

Thrust

Low pressure

Sail

BOAT

Wind direction

High pressure

A yacht sail works like an aircraft wing. When a sail fills with air, it forms the same curved shape as a wing. This changes the flow of air to create low pressure. The low pressure pulls the boat along. It can move a yacht in a different direction from the wind by setting the sails at the correct angle.

WATER BABIES

boats and ships

The biggest and heaviest machines that have ever moved across Earth's surface are ships. Large ships are usually made from steel, while smaller boats are made from wood or plastic.

People have tried building boats from different materials. In 1970, the Norwegian Thor Heyerdahl sailed across the Atlantic Ocean in a boat made from bundles of grass-like reeds tied together!

The carrier produces its own electricity — enough for 100,000 people.

The carrier extracts salt from sea water to make its own fresh water — more than 1.5 million litres every day.

One aircraft carrier costs about £3.2 billion.

PLANE AMAZING!

The US Navy's Nimitz class warships are nuclear-powered floating airports. Each of these ten aircraft carriers is 332 m long, weighs 88,000 tonnes and carries more than 80 aircraft.

MILK FLOAT

Inspired by the milk cartons on his breakfast table, Frank Bölter folded some Tetrapack paper – which is what cartons are often made from – and made a 9-m-long boat. He launched it on the River Elbe in Germany in 2007.

UP AND OVER

One minute it's a ship, the next it's a floating platform for scientists at the Scripps Institute of Oceanography in San Diego, California. Most of the 108-m-long FLIP (Floating Instrument Platform) can be flooded with water to make the stern sink and flip the bow into the air.

BY THE WAY...

During World War II, a British scientist came up with the idea of using a huge aircraft carrier. Although a model keel was built in Canada in 1943, the plan was never built on a lake in Alberta. Still too easy scrapped because the ice.

FLOAT YOUR BOAT

In 1991, archaeologists in Egypt found a fleet of wooden boats, each 18 m long, built nearly 5,000 years ago.

James Castrission and Justin Jones rowed their kayak 3,300 km across the Tasman Sea between Australia and New Zealand. Their voyage took 62 days of paddling up to 18 hours a day.

In March 2003, comedian Tim Fitzhigham rowed a kayak made of paper 257 km down the River Thames. When it leaked during the eight-day journey, he sealed the holes with sticky tape.

In 2003, Robert McDonald from Emmeloord in the Netherlands stayed afloat for 19 minutes in a boat made from 370,000 lollipop sticks.

A regatta held on the Mohawk River near Canajoharie, New York, involves boats made from recycled materials, including plastic milk cartons and bottles.

+twist it!+

UP, UP AND AWAY

balloons

Balloons and airships are actually lighter than air. They contain a gas that weighs less than the air around them. Airships are filled with helium, whereas most balloons are filled with hot air. Hot air is lighter than cold air – that's why smoke floats upwards from a fire.

Airships are powered by engines and propellers, and they can be steered, but balloons drift wherever the wind blows them. Every year, more than 700 balloons take part in the world's biggest balloon festival in Albuquerque, New Mexico.

The first creatures to fly in a hot-air balloon were a rooster, a duck and a sheep in 1783 in France.

MAN POWER

The 46-m-long Action Man that moved through the skies over London claimed to be the world's biggest parachutist balloon.

Ripley explains...

Envelope

Hot air inside balloon

Basket

Burners

Burners above a balloon pilot's head burn propane gas from cylinders in the basket, where the pilot stands. The roaring flame heats the air above it inside the balloon's envelope. The lighter air rises and carries the balloon up with it. The pilot can turn the flame on and off to change the balloon's height above the ground.

BIG BIRD

Balloons can be built in all sorts of shapes, like this eagle. When air is heated by the balloon's gas burners, it expands and fills every part of the eagle.

A LOT OF HOT AIR

At an air base in Chambley, France in 2005, 261 balloons lined up to float into the air at the same time.

World flight

In 1999, Bertrand Piccard and Brian Jones flew the part air-, part helium-filled Breitling Orbiter 3 balloon all the way round the world in one non-stop flight – the first time it had ever been done. The balloon took off in Switzerland, and landed in Egypt.

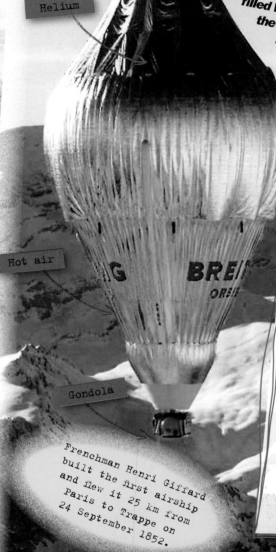

Helium

Hot air

Gondola

The balloon was in the air for 19 days 21 hours 55 minutes and flew a total distance of 46,814 km.

When fully inflated, the balloon stood 55 m tall.

Propane gas fuelled six burners that heated air in the balloon.

The crew travelled inside a sealed capsule, called a gondola, hanging underneath the balloon.

The gondola had flying controls and instruments at one end, a bed in the middle and a toilet at the other end.

Winds blew the balloon along at up to 176 km/h.

Frenchman Henri Giffard built the first airship and flew it 25 km from Paris to Trappe on 24 September 1852.

Ripley's ···· Believe It or Not!®

COUCH LIFT

Kent Couch made a 322-km flight over the state of Orgeon, USA, in 2007 while sitting on a lawn chair. The chair was held aloft by 105 balloons filled with helium. Couch reached a height of 4,267 m and controlled his height by dropping water to go higher or popping balloons to go down. As the wind blew him towards mountains, he popped some balloons and landed in a field near Union, Oregon. The flight lasted 8 hours 45 minutes.

105 balloons

4,267 m up!

CHAIR LIFT

Balloon pilot Pete Dalby floated over Bristol, England, sitting comfortably in an armchair hanging under a hot-air balloon!

SLOW DOWN!

parachutes

When mighty machines get going, it takes a lot of force to stop them. The fastest vehicles sometimes use parachutes to help them slow down. The space shuttle lands at 350 km/h. That's as fast as a racing car at top speed, but the space shuttle weighs a lot more, about 100 tonnes. To help it slow down, a huge 12-m-wide parachute pops out of its tail. It catches so much air that it acts like a brake. Parachutes ease the speed of falling things, too.

The bigger a parachute is — the larger its surface area — the more drag it creates.

Whoa!

The space shuttle orbiter stops with a little help from air resistance, or drag.

Ripley explains...

Canopy

Cells

Lines

A simple round parachute floats straight down, slowed down by air caught underneath it. Most parachutists now use a ram-air canopy that acts a bit like a paraglider. When a ram-air canopy opens, air rushes into pockets called cells sewn into it. The cells filled with air give the parachute the shape of a wing. Instead of coming straight down, it flies like a glider.

HIGH FLIERS

French kitesurfer Sebastien Garat competes in the finals of the Kiteboarding World Championship in Sotavento, Fuerteventura, Spain. Using a wind-filled kite, competitors use the short time between uplift and landing to perform breathtaking acrobatics.

ground control

Safely down, and the parachutes are cut free. The Apollo 11 crew await pickup in their Command Module.

The Apollo 15 Command Module 'Kitty Hawk', with astronauts David R. Scott, Alfred M. Worden and James B. Irwin aboard, nears a safe touchdown in the mid-Pacific Ocean to end their Moon landing mission in 1971. Although causing no harm to the crewmen, one of the three main parachutes failed to function properly.

Don't Let Go!

Skydiver Greg Gasson hangs by just one hand from his parachute strap, high above Eloy, Arizona.

twist it!

WHAT A DRAG

The jet-powered cars that set speed records are so fast that they use a braking parachute to slow down until they reach a speed slow enough for the car's wheel brakes to be used.

DOWNFALL

The Chinese Shenzhou manned spacecraft lands under a parachute big enough to park 100 cars on — 1,200 sq m.

On 16 August 1960, Colonel Joseph W. Kittinger Jr jumped from a balloon at a height of 31,150 m. He fell for 4 minutes 36 seconds before opening his parachute, taking 13 minutes 45 seconds in total to reach the ground.

When Shayna West of Joplin, Missouri, made a parachute jump in 2005, her main and reserve chutes both failed. She fell 3,050 m and landed in a car park, breaking her pelvis, five teeth and several bones in her face. She survived, along with the unborn baby she did not know she was carrying.

When a skydiver in Pittsburgh, USA, caught his foot on the way out of an aircraft door, he dangled from the plane for 30 minutes until it could land. He was unhurt.

Don Kellner from Hazleton, Pennsylvania, has made more than 36,000 skydives. His wife Darlene has made 13,000. They were even married in mid-air by a skydiving minister, Rev. Dave Sangley.

FULL SPEED AHEAD

jet thrust

A jet engine is a big air blower. It blows out a jet of air like a hairdryer, but it blows a lot faster than any hairdryer you've ever used. Air shoots out of a jet engine more than ten times faster than a hurricane and as hot as a blowtorch, so don't ever stand behind a jet engine!

Four of these engines can push a 500-tonne airliner through the air at 900 km/h. Planes aren't the only machines to be powered by jet engines. People have fitted jet engines to boats, cars and even themselves. Jet thrust can also be supplied using water, steam or certain gases.

ENGINE AT THE BACK

Allan Herridge has attached a Viper jet engine to the back of his Volkswagen Beetle. The car has its original 90-horsepower engine at the front, with the 900-kg thrust jet engine at the back. The jet engine can boost the car's speed from 130 km/h to 225 km/h in less than four seconds.

SOLO FLIGHT

This 300 horsepower jet pack enables the wearer to fly at up to 100 km/h and perform tight turns and swoops, soar 9 m up into the air, or hover on the spot. Shooting out two strong jets of water, which provide the thrust, a jet pack flight can last for up to 2 hours.

Sound of mind?

On 15 October 1997, British pilot Andy Green drove a jet-powered car called Thrust SSC faster than the speed of sound. He reached a speed of 1,228 km/h.

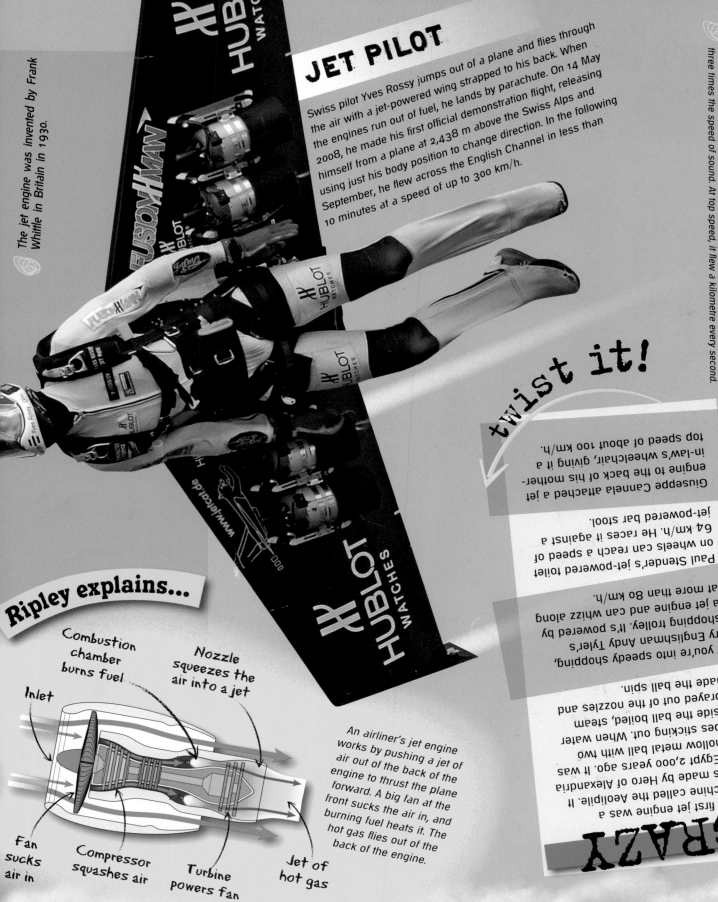

The jet engine was invented by Frank Whittle in Britain in 1930.

JET PILOT

Swiss pilot Yves Rossy jumps out of a plane and flies through the air with a jet-powered wing strapped to his back. When the engines run out of fuel, he lands by parachute. On 14 May 2008, he made his first official demonstration flight, releasing himself from a plane at 2,438 m above the Swiss Alps and using just his body position to change direction. In the following September, he flew across the English Channel in less than 10 minutes at a speed of up to 300 km/h.

twist it!

Giuseppe Cannela attached a jet engine to the back of his mother-in-law's wheelchair, giving it a top speed of about 100 km/h.

Paul Stender's jet-powered toilet on wheels can reach a speed of 64 km/h. He races it against a jet-powered bar stool.

If you're into speedy shopping, try Englishman Andy Tyler's shopping trolley. It's powered by a jet engine and can whizz along at more than 80 km/h.

CRAZY

The first jet engine was a machine called the Aeolipile. It was made by Hero of Alexandria in Egypt 2,000 years ago. It was a hollow metal ball with two pipes sticking out. When water inside the ball boiled, steam sprayed out of the nozzles and made the ball spin.

Ripley explains...

Combustion chamber burns fuel

Nozzle squeezes the air into a jet

Inlet

Fan sucks air in

Compressor squashes air

Turbine powers fan

Jet of hot gas

An airliner's jet engine works by pushing a jet of air out of the back of the engine to thrust the plane forward. A big fan at the front sucks the air in, and burning fuel heats it. The hot gas flies out of the back of the engine.

Thrust SSC was as powerful as 1,000 family cars or 145 Formula 1 racing cars. It was powered by two jet engines from a Phantom fighter.

IN FULL FLIGHT

airliners

Sit back and enjoy the view. You're in an airliner cruising through the sky 10 km above the ground. The clouds are laid out below you like a fluffy white field. They hardly seem to be moving, but you're hurtling through the air at 900 km/h, just below the speed of sound. It's sunny outside, but it's also colder than a deep freeze.

The temperature on the other side of your window could be as low as −60°C, and the air is too thin to breathe. Every year, about 12,000 airliners make more than 15 million flights, carrying more than 2 billion passengers.

An African airline bought a Gulfstream jet for US$4.9 million on the Internet auction site eBay.

Its giant wings measure 79.8 m from tip to tip. They're big enough to park 70 cars on them.

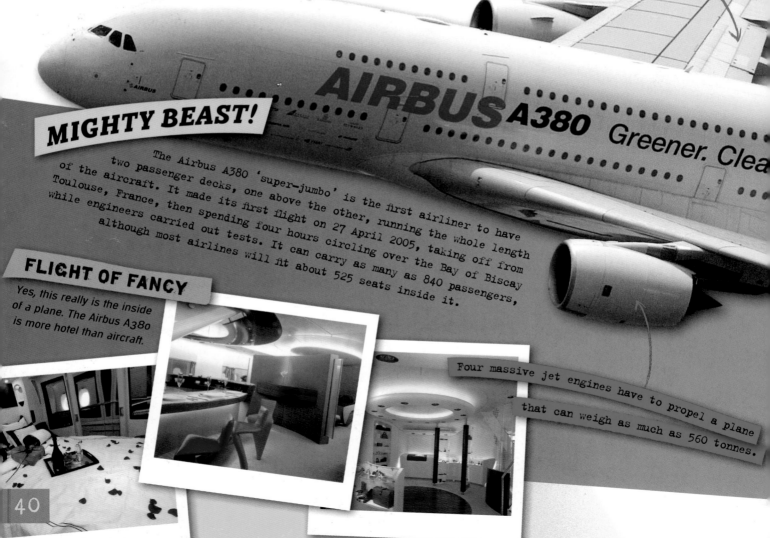

AIRBUS A380 Greener. Clea

MIGHTY BEAST!

The Airbus A380 'super-jumbo' is the first airliner to have two passenger decks, one above the other, running the whole length of the aircraft. It made its first flight on 27 April 2005, taking off from Toulouse, France, then spending four hours circling over the Bay of Biscay while engineers carried out tests. It can carry as many as 840 passengers, although most airlines will fit about 525 seats inside it.

FLIGHT OF FANCY

Yes, this really is the inside of a plane. The Airbus A380 is more hotel than aircraft.

Four massive jet engines have to propel a plane that can weigh as much as 560 tonnes.

CLEARED FOR TAKE-OFF

John Davis spent eight years building an exact copy of a Boeing 747 airliner cockpit in his spare bedroom in his modest home. A 1.8-m screen in front of the cockpit shows views of places from the Alps to New York.

Winglets The Airbus A380 has massive wings – its wingspan is the same as the length of a football pitch. If the wings were the same construction as on other airliners, in order to get the massive Airbus off the ground, they would have to be incredibly long: too long for airports, which all have a maximum wingspan of just 80 m. Designers of the Airbus A380 looked to the wings of an eagle for a solution to the problem.

Here's the science

The tip of an airliner's wing stirs up the air it is moving through. The spinning air stops the wing from working at its best, so the wing has to be made even longer. Designers noticed how an eagle's wingtips curl upwards as it flies. It gave them an idea. They made turned-up wingtips, called winglets for the A380. Each winglet blocks the spinning air and so the wingspan can be kept to 79.8 m.

If five giraffes stood like a tall tower, each one on the head of the one below, they would be the same height as the new Airbus.

The two decks of the 72.75-m-long aircraft cover a surface area of 500 sq m, the equivalent of ten squash courts.

A380

uieter. Smarter.

F-WWOW

5,600 people could stand under the shelter of its wings.

Fuselage

The heavier an aircraft, the more fuel used. The Airbus A380 is longer, wider and has more passengers than any other aircraft, but scientists constructed the outside of the aircraft from an aluminium and fibreglass blend, which is strong yet light.

IN A SPIN

vertical take-off

Hoverflies are little flies that can stay in the same spot in mid-air as if hanging at the end of an invisible thread. Some aircraft can do the same thing. They can take off straight up into the air and hover in one spot. Most of them are helicopters.

Long thin blades on top of a helicopter whirl around hundreds of times a minute, blowing air down like a big fan. The whirling blades blow hard enough to lift a helicopter weighing several tonnes off the ground. There are about 45,000 helicopters in service all over the world. Helicopters have saved more than 3 million lives since the first helicopter rescue in 1944

The tips of the blades whizz round at 730 km/h. The two propellers spin in opposite directions to stop the whole plane from rotating.

Refuelling probe. The Osprey uses this to fill its tanks with fuel from a flying tanker-plane.

The Osprey can carry 24 passengers.

A tail fin provides stability.

MASTER STROKE

Leonardo da Vinci (1452–1519) made a sketch of a flying machine that seems to anticipate the helicopter, though it's not clear how he thought it would work.

WHAT A CHOPPER!   OR IS IT?

The V-22 Osprey takes off like a helicopter. Then its engines and propellers tilt forwards and it flies like a plane. This means it can take off and land almost anywhere, even in remote parts of the world where there is no runway. Built for the military and perfect for use on aircraft carriers, each V-22 Osprey costs about £65 million.

42

Frenchman Gustave de Ponton d'Amécourt invented the word helicopter in 1861.

The Russian Mil Mi-26 is a giant among helicopters. It can carry more than 80 people or 20 tonnes of cargo.

Drive shaft runs through both wings, connecting rotors together, so that if one of the engines breaks down, the other engine will power both propellers.

At speeds of up to 507 km/h, the V-22 Osprey flies twice as fast as a helicopter.

twist it!

In March 2007, a moose that had been shot with a tranquiliser dart near Gustavus, Alaska, charged the hovering helicopter it had been shot from, and brought it down!

In 2005, Frenchman Didier Delsalle landed his helicopter on top of the world's highest mountain, Mount Everest, at a height of 8,848 m.

In 2003, Jonathan Strickland from Inglewood, California, made his first solo flights in a plane and a helicopter on the same day when he was only 14 years of age. He had to go to Canada to do it, because US pilots have to be at least 16 years old.

Alexander van de Rostyne created a tiny helicopter called the Pixelito, weighing only 6.9 grams.

SPIN IT!

uplifting!

Helicopters usually land with ease, but this one had strongman Franz Muellner to contend with. When the 1,800-kg aircraft landed on his shoulders, he managed to hold it off the ground for nearly a minute in Vienna in 2006.

43

BLAST OFF

rocket power

Three... two... one... lift off. If you want to be an astronaut, you'll need a rocket. It's the only way to get into space and it's the boldest, fastest journey you will ever make. The mighty *Saturn V* rocket launched astronauts on their way to the Moon. Today, rocket power takes astronauts to the International Space Station. By the end of 2008, nearly 500 people from 39 countries had hitched a ride on a rocket into space. Rockets blast satellites into orbit too, and they send probes to the Moon and planets. Back here on Earth, smaller firework rockets light up the sky at special events and celebrations.

Ariane 5 can launch satellites weighing up to 10 tonnes.

Each of the two booster rockets weighs 260 tonnes.

Upper stage

ARIANE 5

eutelsat

arianespace
service & solutions

Ariane 5 made its first flight in 1996.

Payload

An Ariane 5 rocket stands 52 m high and at lift-off weighs 780 tonnes.

Ariane 5 rockets launch satellites for the European Space Agency (ESA). They blast off from ESA's spaceport in French Guiana, South America. Ariane 5 is massive. It stands as tall as a 14-story building and weighs as much as 600 cars. It is actually four rockets linked together. The core stage and two booster rockets fire first. When their fuel is used up, they fall away and the upper stage fires to place the cargo in orbit around Earth.

High point

SpaceShipOne rocketed into history in 2004, when it became the first private, manned spacecraft to reach a height of 100 km. In doing this, its team members won the $10-million Ansari X Prize in a competition to encourage civilian spaceflight.

44

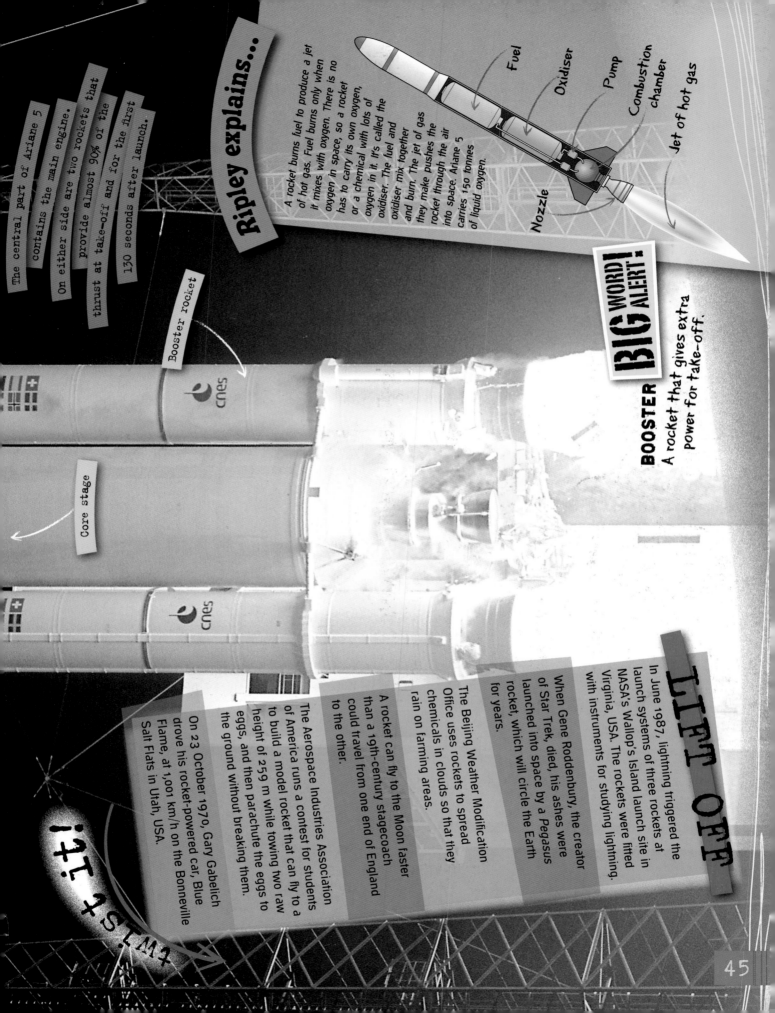

Ripley explains...

The central part of Ariane 5 contains the main engine. On either side are two rockets that provide almost 90% of the thrust at take-off and for the first 130 seconds after launch.

A rocket burns fuel to produce a jet of hot gas. Fuel burns only when it mixes with oxygen. There is no oxygen in space, so a rocket has to carry its own oxygen, or a chemical with lots of oxygen in it. It's called the oxidiser. The fuel and oxidiser mix together and burn. The jet of gas they make pushes the rocket through the air into space. Ariane 5 carries 150 tonnes of liquid oxygen.

Fuel
Oxidiser
Pump
Combustion chamber
Jet of hot gas
Nozzle

BIG WORD ALERT!

BOOSTER
A rocket that gives extra power for take-off.

Booster rocket

Core stage

LIFT OFF

In June 1987, lightning triggered the launch systems of three rockets at launch site in NASA's Wallop's Island launch site in Virginia, USA. The rockets were fitted with instruments for studying lightning.

When Gene Roddenbury, the creator of Star Trek, died, his ashes were launched into space by a Pegasus rocket, which will circle the Earth for years.

The Beijing Weather Modification Office uses rockets to spread chemicals in clouds so that they rain on farming areas.

A rocket can fly to the Moon faster than a 19th-century stagecoach could travel from one end of England to the other.

The Aerospace Industries Association of America runs a contest for students to build a model rocket that can fly to a height of 259 m while towing two raw eggs, and then parachute the eggs to the ground without breaking them.

On 23 October 1970, Gary Gabelich drove his rocket-powered car, Blue Flame, at 1,001 km/h on the Bonneville Salt Flats in Utah, USA.

TEST IT!

MIGHTY MACHINES INDEX

ACKNOWLEDGEMENTS

COVER (l) © Kirill Alperovich – istockphoto.com, (r) Reuters/Ali Jareki; **2** (b) Michael J. Gallagher; **3** (r) Bobby Hunt; **4** (c) Sipa Press/Rex Features; **5** (t/l) © Kirill Alperovich – istockphoto.com; **6** (b/l) Andy Wilman/Rex Features; **6–7** (sp) Photo courtesy of BigFoot 4x4, Inc. © All rights reserved, (bgd) © Eric Gevaert – istockphoto.com; **7** (t/r) Reuters/Ali Jarekji, (b/r) Mike Derer/AP/PA Photos; **8** (b) Rex Features; **8–9** (c) Rex Features; **9** (t/r) Doug Hall/Rex Features, (b) Glenn Roberts, Motorcycle Mojo Magazine/www.motorcyclemojo.com; **10** (c) Reuters/David Mercado; **11** (c) Sean Dempsey/PA Archive/PA Photos, (b) Tina Norris/Rex Features, (r) Bobby Hunt; **12** (sp) Barcroft Media; **13** (r, c/r, b/r) Barcroft Media, (t/l) Patrick Barth/Rex Features, (t/r) Rinspeed; **14** (c) Reuters/Ho New, (b/l) Reuters/Toshiyuki Aizawa; **15** (c) Greg Williams/Rex Features, (b) Joel King/Wrigley's Airwaves ®, (r) Reuters/Sebastian Derungs; **16** Reuters/Reinhard Krause; **17** (t/l) Camera Press, (l) Gavin Bernard/Barcroft Media, (t/c, t/r) Barcroft Media, (b) BP/Barcroft Media; **18** (b/l, sp) Reuters/Tim Wimborne; **19** (l) Courtesy NASA, (b) Jennifer Podis/Rex Features, (t/r) Arko Datta/AFP/Getty Images; **20** (sp) Photo © Harrod Blank; **21** (t) © Duncan Walker – istockphoto.com; **22** (c, t/r) © Bettmann/Corbis; **22–23** (b) Official ISR Photo; **23** (t, t/r) Greg Kolodziejzyk/www.human-power.com, (c/r) Reuters/Anuruddha Lokuhapuarachchi, (b/r) Reuters/Reinhard Krause; **24** (sp/r) Courtesy NASA; **25** (l) Michel Redondo/AP/PA Photos, (c) Michael.J.Gallagher, (t/r) ChinaFotoPress/Photocome/PA Photos; **26** (b/l) Built by Jay Ohrberg/www.jayohrberg.com, (c) Volker Hartmann/AFP/Getty Images; **27** (t/l, l) Copyright © 2006 by Juan Jimenez – Reprinted with permission, (r) Rex Features; **28** (sp) TSGT Joe Zuccaro/AP/PA Photos, (b/r) © John H. Clark/Corbis; **29** (t/l) WENN/Newscom, (b/l) Reuters/Jason Lee, (r) Reuters/Toshiyuki Aizawa; **30** (b/l) Copyright SkySails, (sp) Windstar Cruises; **31** (t/r) Richard Bouhet/AFP/Getty Images, (b) © Photos by Wally Hirsh, corrugated iron sails by Jeff Thomson; **32** (sp) © UPPA/Photoshot; **33** (t/l) Reuters/Christian Charisius, (sp) Bill Call, Scripps Institution of Oceanography, (b/l, b/r) GoldenStateImages.com © Randy Morse; **34** (l) Reuters/Ian Waldie, (r) Reuters/Denis Balibouse; **35** (l) Reuters/Stringer France, (c) © Fabrice Coffrini/epa/Corbis, (b/l) South West News/Rex Features, (b/r) Pete Erickson/AP/PA Photos; **36** (t) Rex Features, (b/r) © Carlos De Saa/epa/Corbis; **37** (t/l) Joe Jennings/Barcroft Media, (b) Reuters/Dan Chung, (t/c, t/r) Courtesy NASA; **38–39** (b) Michael Sohn/AP/PA Photos; **38** (r) Jetlev-flyer.com/Solent News/Rex Features, (r) Harry How/Allsport/Getty Images; **39** (c) Fabrice Coffrini/AFP/Getty Images; **40–41** (dp) Reuters/Charles Pertwee; **40** (b/l) Camera Press/David Dyson, (b/c, b/r) ©Airbus 2004 Camera Press/ED/RA; **41** (t, t/r) David Burner/Rex Features; **42** (r) Mary Evans Picture Library, (l) David Jones/PA Archive/PA Photos, (r) Gerry Bromme/AP/PA Photos; **43** (r) Vladimir Kmet/AFP/Getty Images; **44–45** (dp) ESA/CNES/Arianespace/Service Optique Video du CSG; **44** (l, r) Reuters/Mike Blake

Key: t = top, b = bottom, c = centre, l = left, r = right, sp = single page, dp = double page, bgd = background

All other photos are from Ripley Entertainment Inc.

All artwork by Dynamo Design

Every attempt has been made to acknowledge correctly and contact copyright holders and we apologise in advance for any unintentional errors or omissions, which will be corrected in future editions.